Images of
FLANDERS
THE GREAT WAR IN
YPRES

La Cathédrale Saint-Martin.

La Cathédrale Saint-Martin I.

La Porte de Menin.

Souvenir d' Ypres.

Les Halles III. Le Nieuwerck. 1620.

La Petite Conciergerie, rebâtie en 1633.

Hospice Belle.

Les Halles I.

La Cathédrale Saint-Martin.
Portail méridional.

Les Remparts, près de la Station.

Panorama.

Les Halles. II. La Salle échevinale.

Images of
FLANDERS
THE GREAT WAR IN
YPRES

Jacky Platteeuw

TEMPUS

First published 2005

Tempus Publishing Limited
The Mill, Brimscombe Port,
Stroud, Gloucestershire, GL5 2QG
www.tempus-publishing.com

British Library Cataloguing in Publication Data.
A catalogue record for this book is available from the British Library.

ISBN 90-76684-52-9
NUR: 520
Wettelijk depot: D/2005/8557/116

Typesetting and origination by Tempus Publishing Limited.
Printed in Great Britain.

Contents

Acknowledgements

The author wishes to thank everybody who provided photographs for this book, or helped in any way in its making, with particular thanks to: Stadsarchief (Ypres), In Flanders Fields Documentatiecentrum (Ypres), Freddy Bauwen (Ypres), Roland Meulebroeck (Ypres), Paul Reed (Canterbury), Genevra Charsley (Ypres) and Aurel Sercu (Boezinge).

Place-names

In the book we have often used the Dutch names of places, streets and buildings. For reference there is a list on pages 127 and 128 with the English and French translations. One exception is in the name of the town itself, where we have preferred the French 'Ypres' above the Dutch 'Ieper' because the French name is better known in English.

Introduction

During the Great War thousands of soldiers from all corners of the British Isles and the Commonwealth fought and lost their lives on the battlefields of the Ypres Salient in the west of Belgium, near the French border.

The soldiers names are engraved in stone in numerous cemeteries and on memorials. For more than seventy-five years the Last Post has been sounded every evening at the Menin Memeorial Gate, a ceremony by which the town wishes to express its gratitude for all the soldiers' sacrifices. The ceremony takes place amidst the infinite rows of names of the soldiers who went missing in the Great War.

Through photographs and postcards, we would like this book to give the reader an idea of three different periods in Ypres: before, during and after the Great War.

The selection of photographs was difficult as there is much material available. We have tried to share with you, through a personal selection, the views and images of this sad episode in European history.

Jacky Platteeuw

Souvenir d' Ypres.

1

Before the Great War

Panorama taken from St Maartenskathedraal around 1910.

A rooftop view of Ypres, taken from the water tower originally situated in today's Maarschalk Haiglaan.

The Grote Markt on the east side, with the hospitaal on the left. In front of it is a permanent bandstand.

The Grote Markt on the west side. On the left is the Hallen and on the right is St Maartenskathedraal. The Hallen is a very large Cloth Hall that was built between 1260 and 1304, when ships on the now vaulted River Ieperlee adjacent to it could sail right into the Hall to unload their cargo.

The weekly market on Saturday has always been and still is an important event for the city, not only from an economical point of view but also as an interesting spot to meet and catch up on the latest local news and gossip.

Detailed view of the Hallen and the west side of the Grote Markt.

The Pauwels room in the Hallen was named after the painter of the frescos on the walls. They glorify the history of Ypres and Flanders. This beautiful room was never restored after the war.

A close-up from Nieuwerck, an extension of the Hallen. Built between 1620 and 1623, it replaced a wooden structure.

The Vleeshuis or Groot Vleeshuis, dating from the 13th century, was used as a municipal museum from 1858 onwards.

A. Vandenpeereboomplein, named after Alphonse Vandenpeereboom (1812-1884), a former Minister and Mayor. In the foreground is a statue in tribute to him and in the background is the Parnassushof, today's Stadsschouwburg.

St Maartenskathedraal dates from the 13th century (1221-1280).

The north side of the A. Vandenpeereboomplein with the Kloosterpoort to the right of the picture.

Detail of the Kloosterpoort, built in a very Classical style.

An old Gothic façade in Elverdingsestraat.

The prison in Elverdingsestraat was built between 1873 and 1876.

Stationsplein, built around 1900 after the completion of the western ramparts.

The railway station, unveiled in 1900.

Exterior of the railway station, constructed in a modern style with the use of much metal.

Maloulaan was built around the same period as the railway station.

St Niklaaskerk in Gustaaf De Steursstraat made its first appearance in the archives around 1180. The church on the right of the picture was completed in 1854.

Two old taverns on Gustaaf de Steursstraat: the Ville de Pekin (Town of Peking) and the Grand Tivoli (Great Tivoli).

19

A general view of Gustaaf De Steursstaat, named after an ex-alderman and great benefactor of the city.

Boterstraat is one of the commercial veins of Ypres. This is a view towards the Grote Markt.

Neptunuspoort (Neptune's Gate) is commonly called Vispoort (Fish Gate). The sculpture, representing the god Neptune riding a sea horse and holding a trident, is by Maurice Deraedt and was unveiled in 1714.

The Vismarkt with the Minkhuis constructed in 1899.

Boomgaardstraat, with a view on the back of Vleeshuis.

A more general view of Boomgaardstraat.

A view along Rijselsestraat pointing towards the north; in the background are the Hallen and St Maartenskathedraal.

Façade of Belle Godshuis in Rijselsestraat.

The Hotel Museum Merghelynck on the corner of Rijselsestraat and Merghelynckstraat is named after Arthur Merghelynck, a town archivist.

The Tempeliersteen in Rijselsestraat housed the post office. This photograph represents the building after 1898.

A view along Rijselsestraat south towards St Pieterskerk.

Detailed view of St Pieterskerk. The parish of St Pieter was first mentioned in 1073 and is the oldest parish of Ypres.

View taken from Rijselsepoort to Rijselsestraat.

Hospice Nazareth was built in 1336. It served as a home for the poor and elderly for many years until it was recently converted to house the police.

Rijselsepoort dates back to the 14th century. In Dutch it is also called the Mecinpoort (Messines Gate).

The Houten Huis (wooden house) near the Rijselsepoort was one of the last surviving Middle Age houses in Ypres.

Outside view of the Rijselsepoort.

The Rijselsepoort with the *vestingen* or ramparts constructed in the 17th century by Vauban, a famous French defence builder.

DHondtstraat with Hotel de Gand, one of the few hotels in Ypres before the war.

St Jacobskerk was first mentioned as a chapel at the end of the 11th century. The church was constructed at the end of the 14th century.

The Menenpoort. On both sides of the gate stood a lion, both of which were donated to the Australian Government after the Great War. To this day they are on display in the Australian War Memorial at Canberra.

The Oude Houtmarkt, also known as Oude Beestenmarkt.

An old façade in Diksmuidsestraat.

A more general view of Diksmuidsestraat.

31

The Veemarkt, commonly known as Beestenmarkt.

The guildhalls on the
Veemarkt.

The Kaai, a small harbour on the Ypres-IJzer Canal. This canal was of great strategic importance during the Great War and it was one of the few natural defences the Allies had.

The north side of Nieuwerck and part of the Janseniusstraat. This street was named after theologian Jansenius, a famous Bishop and founder of Jansenism.

Rear view of St Maartenskathedraal.

Ypres had a very flourishing lace production trade before the war, but like many other trades it disappeared after the war.

2

During the Great War

A very common view of the Great War: fugitives fleeing the violence. The photographs and postcards in this chapter will illustrate how difficult it is to describe the tragedy which happened in Flanders' Fields in words; often the images speak for themselves.

BRITISH GIFTS FOR   BELGIAN SOLDIERS

La
GRANDE BRETAGNE
ACCUEILLE
les
RÉFUGIÉS
BELGES

En
GREAT BRITAIN
WELCOMES
the
BELGIAN
REFUGEES

By
ANDRÉ CLUYSENAAR

Propaganda became part of the experience of war, here we have a bilingual postcard welcoming soldiers and refugees of *Brave Little Belgium*; Britain embraces the Belgians.

LES VILLES MARTYRES
YPRES *(LES HALLES)*

The Martyred Cities were a well-known theme of Allied propaganda and Ypres played an important role there. Mostly the burning Hallen were represented.

Belgian soldiers trying to make the best of it.

To think that the war had only just started... Looking at these men one can't help wondering how many survived.

This photograph and the five following really speak for themselves. They are a testimony of the human madness which destroyed a beautiful town and reduced it to ruins.

An aerial view of the Grote Markt and surroundings.

The destruction of the Grote Markt.

The A. Vandenpeereboomplein with St Maartenskathedraal and Kloosterpoort.

Above and below: Two ground-level views depicting the destruction of Ypres.

The Hallen in 1915.

British troops passing the Hallen on their way to the Front (1915).

Troops passing through Grote Markt during the winter of 1917.

The remains of the Hallen towards the end of the war, nothing more than a pile of rubble and a shell of a façade.

The south side of the Grote Markt showed no great damage in 1914; a few months later the site would present an entirely different picture.

St Maartenskathedraal and the north side of Grote Markt around the end of 1914 or early 1915.

Almost the same spot a few months later.

Boomgaardstraat in 1915.

The rear of Vleeshuis in Boomgaardstraat in 1915, with the Hallen in the middle.

A. Vandenpeereboomplein in 1915.

A more detailed view of part of
A. Vandenpeereboomplein. The sign of the
Boerenhol tavern is still visible.

St Maartenskathedraal in 1916.

Rijselsestraat towards St Pieterskerk in 1915.

Rijselsestraat towards Hallen and St Maartenskathedraal in 1915.

Above: Two views of the Belfort: to the left in 1915 and on the right in early 1916.

Left: The rear side of Belle Godshuis in Rijselsestraat.

The heavy construction of the infantry barracks of Ypres offered some protection against artillery fire.

The Riding School of Ypres was world-famous before the war. It was never re-opened after the war.

Desolation all around Rijselsepoort.

The mutilated ramparts that were once the pride of Ypres. In the foreground is a temporary bridge.

Concrete shelters on the ramparts.

The prison in the Elverdingsestraat with a few Tommies in front of it.

The ruins in Elverdingsestraat.

The same desolation in the G. De Steursstraat.

The remains of St Niklaaskerk.

The railway station in ruins.

Not much is left of this platform of the railway station.

A vehicle passes through the barricaded Menenpoort.

3

After the Great War

In this chapter the ruins are the focal point once again, with a particularly impressive series of photographs taken in February 1919. The snow tries to cover the sad story of the ruins, the rubble disappears under the white innocence of the snow and only the silent skeletons of a once lively town tell of what took place here during four long years. Nevertheless, the second part of this chapter is one full of hope: the reconstruction of the town becomes a reality and normal life slowly returns.

The Belgian lion has crushed the German eagle. The caption of this postcard says it all: 'Free at last'. Once again Ypres with its destroyed Hallen is one of the featured martyred cities.

February 1919. Winter on the ruins: snow has spread its mantle over the town.

A general view of Ypres.

Grote Markt in 1919.

February 1919: Hallen.

February 1919: Grote Markt and St Maartenskathedraal.

February 1919: a hospital on the east side of Grote Markt.

The ruins of the Belfort. A sign warns about unexploded ordnance.

February 1919: St Maartenskathedraal and A. Vandenpeereboomplein.

St Maartenskathedraal.

February 1919: the front entrance of St Maartenkathedraal.

General view of A.Vandenpeereboomplein.

February 1919: Kloosterpoort on the A.Vandenpeereboomplein.

February 1919: Nieuwe Houtmarkstraat and the corner of Beestenmarkt.

February 1919: Elverdingsestraat.

Interior of the prison (Elverdingsestraat). In the entrance a wooden sign: Receiving Room for Wounded.

February 1919: the asylum for the mentally ill on the Poperingseweg.

The stationplein in February 1919.

February 1919: G. De Steursstraat.

Note the two civilians near St Niklaaskerk. Normal life is slowly returning.

Boterstraat.

February 1919: Boterstraat.

Rijselsestraat in February 1919.

68

February 1919: the ruins of the post office in Rijselsestraat.

St Pieterskerk in Rijselsestraat, February 1919.

February 1919: Rijselsepoort.

February 1919: remains of trenches on the fortifications.

February 1919: St Jacobskerk.

The interior of St Jacobskerk.

February 1919: DHondtstraat.

February 1919: Diksmuidsestraat.

Scaffolding appears at the start of what is to be the reconstruction of Ypres.

Detail of the Hallen.

Above and below: After the war, life goes on. These photographs show the contrast between making a new start and not forgetting the past. Above: a fair in August 1921 where the ruins make a bizarre background for the *friture* (chips shop) and the merry-go-rounds. Below: the *Fête des Invalides* in 1922, with the ruins serving as background to a Commemoration of the Wounded. The Albert houses, temporary wooden houses, are emerging, in the distance.

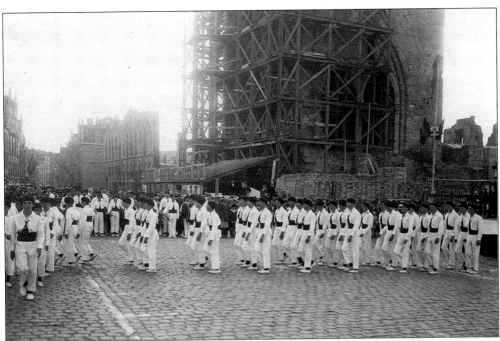

A gymnastic event on the Grote Markt in the late 1920s. The Hallen still has scaffolding surrounding it but in the background Boterstraat has already taken the shape we know today.

Hope for a better future: the people of Ypres are proudly presenting a model of their Belfort.

The Grote Markt on the north side is already partly rebuilt. St Maartenskathedraal is still in scaffold but rising steadily.

An impressive view of the rebuilding of St Maartenskathedraal.

Sculptors creating elements for St Maartenskathedraal.

A group of stonemasons pose for the camera. A child has proudly marked his daddy (*papa* in Dutch) with a cross.

Stonemasons working at the Hallen.

G. De Steurstraat in 1921. The town of Ypres is about to receive the Military Cross. The so-called Nissen huts, well known to the troops, are used all around town to give shelter to returned civilians.

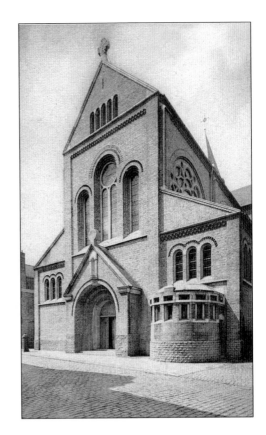

Reconstructed St Niklaaskerk.

The famous Albert houses were named after the Belgian King. They were easy to construct and gave shelter to many families in Ypres after the war.

Boterstraat in the late 1920s. The Hallen on the left is still in scaffolding. To the right St Jacobskerk is almost finished.

Boterstraat with the law court in the background, built on the east side of Grote Markt where the old hospital stood before the Great War.

Vismarkt and reconstructed Minkhuis.

Rijselsestraat in 1923.

Another view of Rijselsestraat in 1923.

The Belfort in the late 1930s, unveiled in 1934. St Maartenskathedraal was rebuilt in a totally different style from before the war.

The work on the Hallen is still ongoing and a new part is in construction.

The Hallen are finished, only Nieuwerck is still to be rebuilt. The photograph dates from the early 1950s.

He would make a good equilibrist…

St Jacobskerk almost finished.

Guido Gezelleplein near St Jacobskerk is named after a famous Flemish poet.

Meensestraat. In the background the construction of the Menenpoort is underway.

Maarschalk Frenchlaan, situated on the Menin road just outside the Menenpoort.

St Pieterskerk is rebuilt in a completely
new style.

Panorama of Ypres in the late 1950s. The phoenix has risen from the ashes.

Another panoramic view from the late 1950s.

The Munstercross, colloquially known as *Iers kruis* (Irish Cross) situated behind St Maartenskathedraal in the Janseniusstraat.

Graves scattered about in the landscape were a typical view of the Ypres Salient shortly after the Great War.

Ypres Reservoir Cemetery as it was directly after the war, with wooden crosses.

The same cemetery in the 1960s. The wooden crosses have been replaced by uniform headstones, with the message being very clear: in death everyone is equal.

A ceremony of remembrance in Ypres Reservoir Cemetery in the late 1920s. Here the Lord Mayor of London pays his respects to the fallen.

Remparts Cemetery near Rijselsepoort is an oasis of peace. A calm and quiet atmosphere surrounds this particular spot allowing one to pause for a moment of reflection.

Another photograph taken from outside Rijselsepoort.

Menin Road South Cemetery on the way to Hell Fire Corner, considered to be one of the most infamous spots of the whole of the Western Front during the war.

Ruins in Ypres used as a Memorial.

The pilgrimage of the Royal British Legion in 1928, considered to be the biggest pilgrimage ever, with some 11,000 people attending.

The Royal Britsh Legion in 1928, with standards of the different branches.

The Royal Britsh Legion in 1928.

The Royal Britsh Legion in 1928. Note Prince Edward in the parade.

The Royal Britsh Legion in 1928.

One of the numerous commemoration ceremonies held in Ypres between the First and the Second World War.

The visit of the Lord Mayor of London, Sir Charles Batho, on 22 April 1928. The gentleman to the left is Pierre Vandenbraambussche, founder of the Last Post Association. This Association is responsible for the sounding of the Last Post every night at the Menin Gate.

Mayor Sobry of Ypres inspecting cadets of the Durham Light Infantry on the Grote Markt.

The Monument to the Belgian fallen on the A. Vandenpeereboomplein.

Mayor Sobry talking to Lady Haig in front of the Belgian Monument.

The same ceremony with a more general view of the reconstructed A. Vandenpeereboomplein.

Visit of Lord Galway, Governor General of New Zealand, on 23 Feburary 1935.

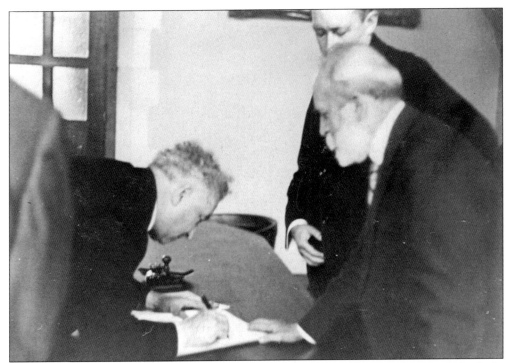

Visit by British Members of Parliament on 9 July 1938, seen here signing the visitors book. In the middle of the table a Toc-H lamp is visible. The lamp is the lamp of maintenance adopted by Toc-H, a charitable organisation, and has on it the Cross of Ypres which Toc-H has been given permission to use.

On 28 July 1946, the British Ambassador came to present a standard to the Royal British Legion Ypres Branch.

View of the rear side of the Excelsior Hotel on the Grote Markt. Hallen and St Maartenskathedraal are still in ruins. This photograph is from the early 1920s.

A front view of the Excelsior Hotel with cars and a bus parked in front of it: the beginning of the battlefield pilgrimages and war tourism.

Although Ypres had welcomed some tourists before the Great War, after the Great War the numbers of people visiting the sites where beloved once had fought or where buried grew enormously. Here we see buses waiting next to the Ypriana Hotel, situated just outside Menenpoort.

The Flandria Hotel and restaurant situated on Maarschalk Frenchlaan, between the Menenpoort and Meenseweg.

YPRES — Porte de Menin
Baraque reconstruite au milieu des ruines.
Hotel Restaurant.

The Café des Touristes and annexed garage, one of the first in Ypres, was situated outside the Menenpoort.

YPRES — Porte de Menin.
Au nouveau Téléphone. Restaurant Henri Knockaerts. Première baraque réédifiée au milieu des ruines.

The restaurant In de Nieuwe Telefoon, just outside the Menenpoort: still a barrack, but with tiles on the roof. The restaurant was frequented by local customers and many Commonwealth soldiers also went there for a meal.

The Ypriana Hotel situated in the Maarschalk Frenchlaan.

On the back of this photograph is written 'Ypres', however this pub is unknown,. This is not unusual, considering that such places often sprung up out of nowhere in Ypres and then just as quickly disappeared.

Another establishment appearing in Ypres – not particularly 'Royal' looking by any stretch of the imagination!

The Boomgaardstraat and the shop of Mr Murphy, one of the first people to open a museum on the Salient. He also organised visits to the old battlefields.

The British Tavern on the Grote Markt was a temporary wooden structure. This particular one was painted in blue and therefore somewhat distinguishable.

The name of this building on the Grote Markt says it all: Splendid and British!

Haigs House, a charity fund, was active in Ypres between 1932 and 1948. The club house was situated in Korte Torhoutstraat, where this photograph was taken around 1935.

The Excelsior Hotel on the Grote Markt developed in the 1930s from a temporary house to this magnificent building.

Hotel Sultan on the Grote Markt, a famous hotel that still exists and has even kept its name.

The signboard on this tea room on the Grote Markt hasn't changed at all and can still be seen today.

Café de L'ancre on the Grote Markt around 1930.

On the right: Skindles restaurant situated near the railway station in Ypres. On the left is the very well known hotel with the same name of Skindles in Poperinge.

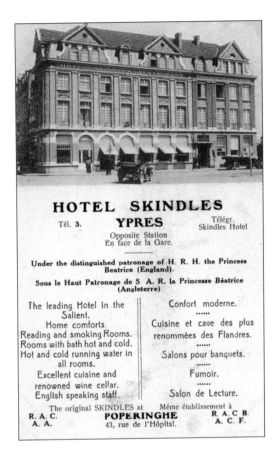

HOTEL SKINDLES

Tél. **3.** **YPRES** Télégr.
Skindles Hotel

Opposite Station
En face de la Gare.

Under the distinguished patronage of H. R. H. the Princess
Beatrice (England).

Sous le Haut Patronage de S. A. R. la Princesse Béatrice
(Angleterre)

The leading Hotel in the Salient.	Confort moderne.
Home comforts.	......
Reading and smoking Rooms.	Cuisine et cave des plus renommées des Flandres.
Rooms with bath hot and cold.	......
Hot and cold running water in all rooms.	Salons pour banquets.
Excellent cuisine and renowned wine cellar.	......
	Fumoir.
English speaking staff.	......
	Salon de Lecture.

The original SKINDLES at   Même établissement à
R. A. C.   **POPERINGHE**   R. A. C. B.
A. A.   43, rue de l'Hôpital.   A. C. F.

Skindles Hotel at René Colaertplein
(former Place de la Gare).

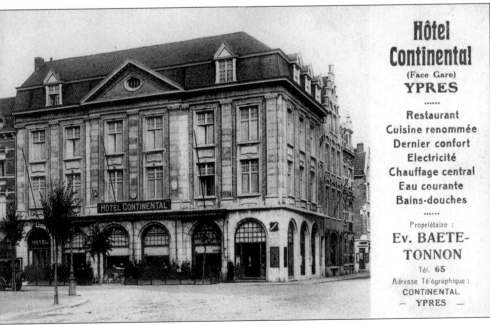

Hôtel Continental

(Face Gare)

YPRES

......

Restaurant
Cuisine renommée
Dernier confort
Electricité
Chauffage central
Eau courante
Bains-douches

......

Propriétaire :

Ev. BAETE-TONNON

Tél. 65

Adresse Télégraphique :
CONTINENTAL
— YPRES —

The Continental Hotel on the opposite side of Skindles.

The Cosmopolite Hotel has now gone, but its façade can still be seen in Stationsstraat 62. Photograph taken c. 1925.

In the same Stationsstraat the Universal Hotel was to be found. Today the façade can still be seen at no. 15.

Hotel de La Gare was one of the many hotels situated around the railway station.

O. BUSSCHAERT - VAN DEN BOSCH
ARTICLES DE TOILETTE
Place de la Gare — YPRES

Local people quickly adapted to the situation: here a hairdresser on René Colaertplein has started selling postcards and souvenirs as well.

Blue Queen's Excursions

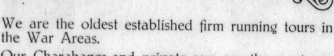

We are the oldest established firm running tours in the War Areas.

Our Charabancs and private cars are the most up-to-date and the most luxurious to be found on the Belgian coast.

Our Drivers and Guides are bona fide British ex-servicemen.

We run daily excursions to the Battle Fields, Ypres and Hill 60, Brussels, Antwerp, Ghent and Bruges, and weekly excursions, on Thursdays, to Middelburg Market (Holland).

Special arrangements for large parties.

Photot Industr. Belge, 83-85, r Etangs-Noirs, Brux — Tél. 670,61.

Above and below: Blue Queen's Cars recommend their excursions to the old battlefields: the ruins of Ypres have become a curiosity.

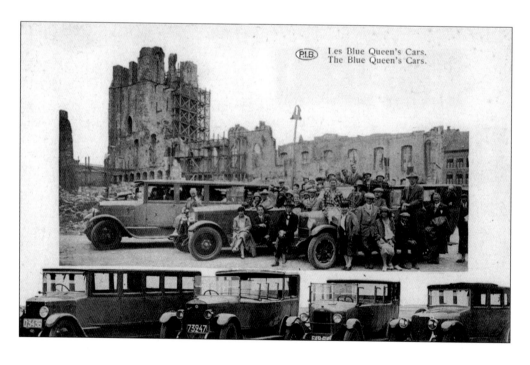

Les Blue Queen's Cars.
The Blue Queen's Cars.

The first Ypres Salient Museum was located in the basement of Vleeshuis.

René Colaertplein, with a sign 'Battlefield Tours' above the three people in the middle.

The new railway station.

The famous relic of a British tank at René Colaertplein right in front of the railway station. The Germans melted it down during the Second World War.

Tourists posing in front of a 21cm German gun at René Colaertplein in 1933.

The same gun in detail.

The first stone of St George's Memorial Church was laid by Field Marshall French on 24 July 1927.

St George's Memorial Church in detail.

Greeting card with some typical views.

The Menin Gate Memorial is a Hall of Memory constructed at the site of Menin Gate, one of Ypres' gateways that was a mere passage when so many passed through it on their way to the trenches. Field Marshal Plumer unveiled the Memorial on 24 July 1927. The large Hall was designed by Sir Reginald Blomfield, one of the four principal architects who were engaged by the Commonwealth War Graves Commission to supervise the construction of over 1,200 cemeteries and memorials along the Western Front. In his memoirs, Sir Blomfield, who also designed the Cross of Sacrifice, stated that the Menin Gate was the only building he was completely satisfied with. The Memorial, built of reinforced concrete faced with Euville stone and red brick, is 36.5 metres long and 20 metres wide. The names of almost 55,000 soldiers who went missing in action are engraved in stone panels fixed to the inner walls of the Hall, up the sides of the staircases and inside the loggias.

In the photograph above, the Menenpoort is almost finished.

The first step: the foundations are completed.

A view of the works from Meensestraat.

An aerial view of the Menenpoort.

Above and right: Two photographs of the unveiling of the Menenpoort on 24 July 1927.

An aerial view of the great pilgrimage by the Royal British Legion on 8 August 1928.

The crowd during the ceremony.

About 11,000 people participated in the Royal British Legion pilgrimage of 1928.

A view from inside the Menenpoort towards the Grote Markt with the Hallen in the middle of the picture.

A common view at the Menenpoort: pilgrims or tourists taking a souvenir photograph.

A photograph taken in the 1930s after a Last Post Ceremony.

Hommage to the fallen.

Former President of the United States Herbert Hoover visiting the Menenpoort on 16 February 1938.

The Menenpoort during the Second World War, part of the bridge has been blown up by British Engineers.

A Last Post Ceremony during the 1950s.

List of place-names

A. Merghelynckstraat	Rue A. Merghelynck	A. Merghelynckstreet
A. Vandenpeereboomplein	Place A. Vandenpeereboom	A.Vandenpeereboom square
Beestenmarkt	Marché au betail	Cattlemarket
Belfort	Beffroi	Belfry
Belle Godshuis	Hospice Belle	Belle Hospice
Biebuyckhuis	Maison Biebuyck	Biebuycks House
Boomgaardstraat	Rue du Verger	Orchardstreet
Boterstraat	Rue au Beurre	Butterstreet
DHondtstraat	Rue DHondt	DHondtstreet
Diksmuidesestraat	Rue de Dixmude	Diksmuidestreet
Elverdingsestraat	Rue dElverdinge	Elverdingestreet
Gustaaf De Steursstraat	Rue G. De Steurs	G. De Steursstreet
Gevangenis	Prison	Prison
Grote Markt	Grande Place	Square
Guido Gezelleplein	Place Guido Gezelle	Guid Gezelle Square
Hallen	Les Halles	Cloth Hall
Hospitaal	Hôpital	Hospital
Houten Huis	Maison de bois	Wooden House
Ypres	Ypres	Ypres
Janseniusstraat	Rue Jansenius	Janseniusstreet
Kaai	Quai	Quay
Kloosterpoort	Porte du Cloitre	Cloister Gate
Korte Torhoutstraat	Rue Courte de Torhout	Short Torhoutstreet
Maarschalk Frenchlaan	Avenue Maréchal French	Field Marshall French Avenue
Maarschalk Haiglaan	Avenue Marechal Haig	Field Marshall Haig Avenue
Maloulaan	Avenue Malou	Malou Avenue
Meensestraat	Rue de Menin	Meninstreet
Menenpoort	Porte de Menin	Menin Gate
Merghelynckmuseum	Musée Merghelynck	Merghelynck Museum
Nazareth	Hospice Nazareth	Nazareth Hospice
Neptunuspoort of Vispoort	Porte Neptune	Neptune's Gate
Nieuwerck	Nieuwerck	Nieuwerck
Oude Houtmarkt	Marché au Bois	Woodmarket

Poperingseweg	Rue de Poperinghe	Poperingeroad
Post	La Poste	Post Office
René Colaertplein	Place René Colaert	René Colaert Square
Rijselsepoort	Porte de Lille	Lille Gate
Rijselsestraat	Rue de Lille	Lillestreet
St Jacobskerk	Eglise St Jacques	St James' Church
St Maartenskathedraal	Cathédrale St Martin	St Martin's Cathedral
St Niklaaskerk	Eglise St Nicolas	St Nicolas' Church
St Pieterskerk	Eglise St Pierre	St Peter's Church
Stadsschouwburg	Théâtre Municipal	Municipal Theatre
Station	Gare	Railway station
Stationsplein	Place de la Gare	Railway square
Stationsstraat	Rue de la Gare	Stationstreet
Tempelierssteen of Hooghuis	Maison des Templiers	Templars House
Veemarkt	Marché au betail	Cattlemarket
Vestingen	Remparts	Ramparts
Vismarkt	Marché aux Poissons	Fishmarket
Vleeshal of Groot Vleeshuis	La Boucherie	Butchers Hall